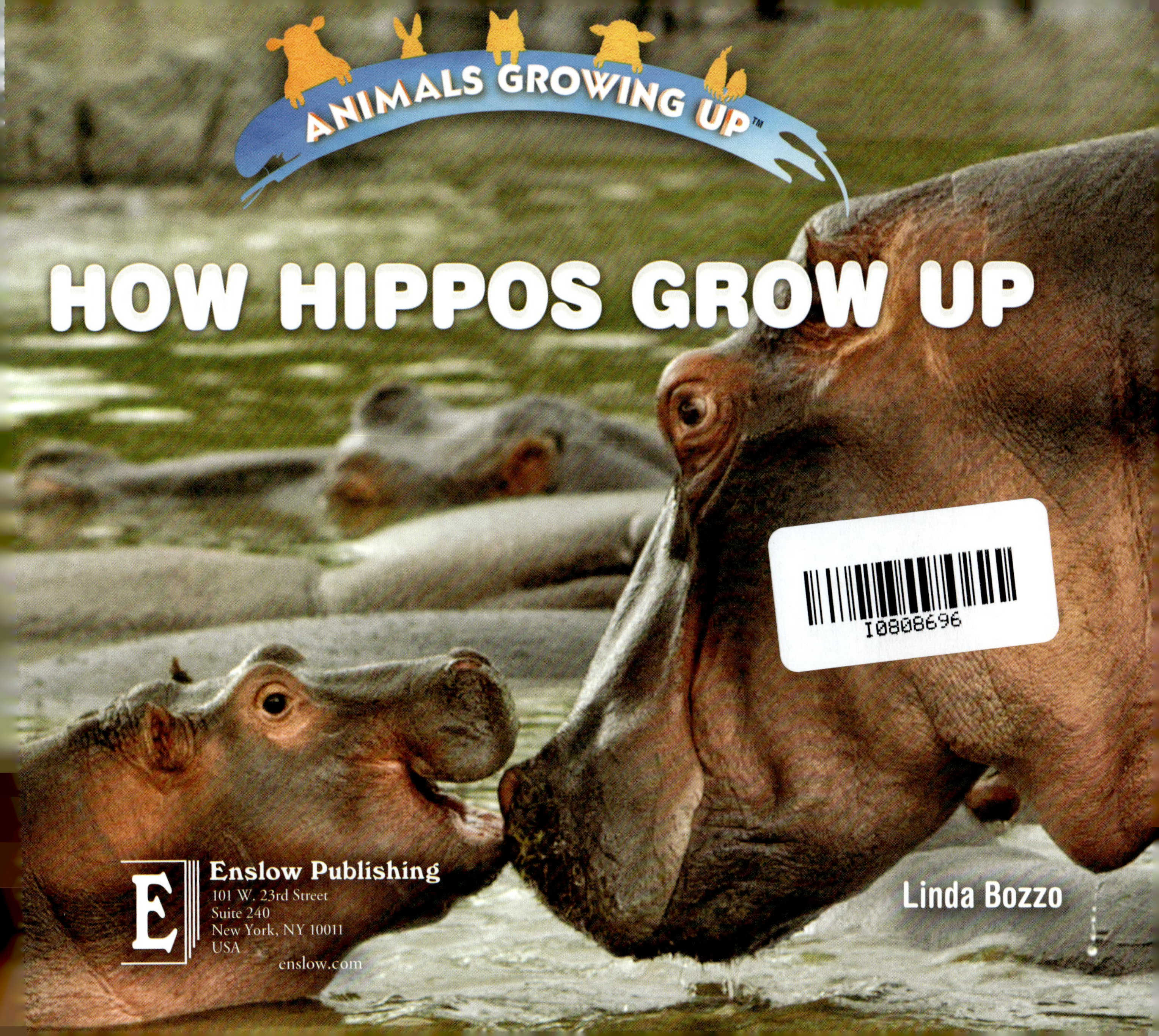

ANIMALS GROWING UP™

HOW HIPPOS GROW UP

Linda Bozzo

Enslow Publishing
101 W. 23rd Street
Suite 240
New York, NY 10011
USA
enslow.com

WORDS TO KNOW

breed To have babies.

calf A baby hippo.

cow A mother hippo.

graze To eat grass and other plants growing in a field.

herd A large group of adult and young hippos that live together.

nurse To drink milk from the mother's body.

predator An animal that kills and eats other animals to live.

shallow Not deep.

wallow To roll around in mud or water.

CONTENTS

BIG BABIES

A baby hippo is called a **calf**. Calves are big babies! They can weigh as much as 100 pounds (45 kilograms) when they are born.

A hippo will only have one baby every two years.

FAST FACT

"Hippopotamus" is a big word, so most people say "hippo" instead.

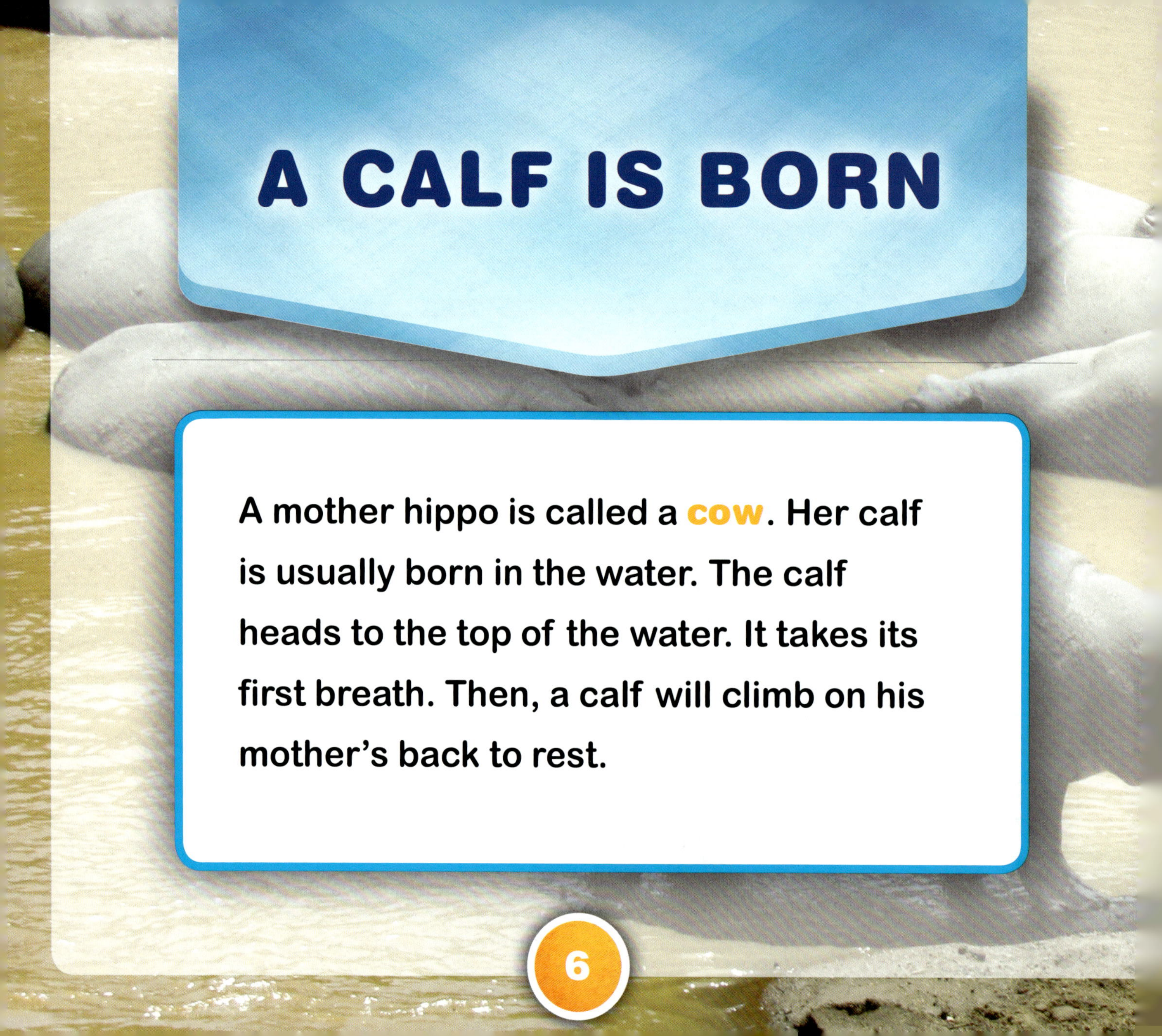

A CALF IS BORN

A mother hippo is called a **cow**. Her calf is usually born in the water. The calf heads to the top of the water. It takes its first breath. Then, a calf will climb on his mother's back to rest.

FAST FACT

Hippos are too heavy to swim. They walk underwater and bounce to the surface.

Hippos close their ears and noses underwater to keep water out.

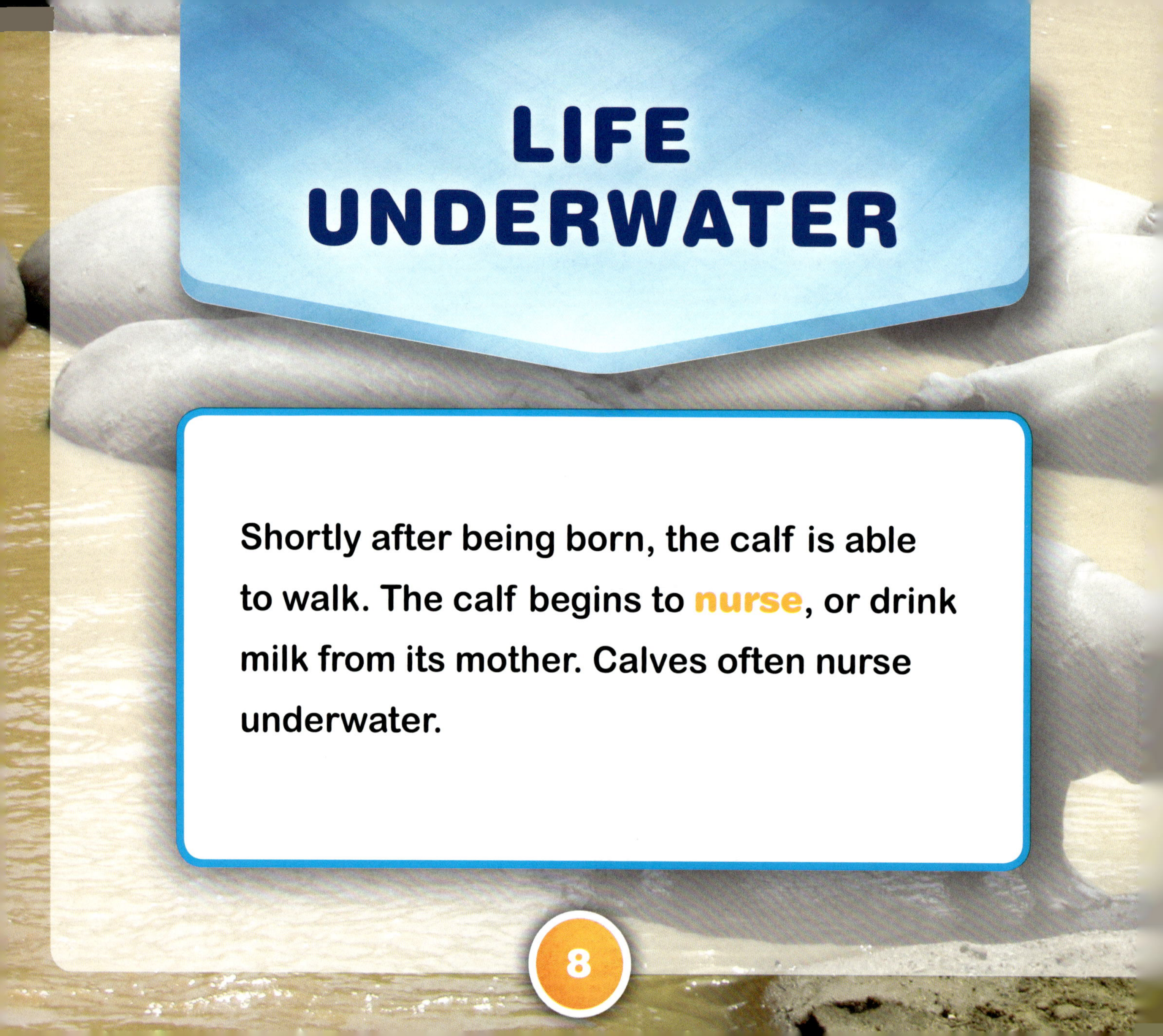

LIFE UNDERWATER

Shortly after being born, the calf is able to walk. The calf begins to **nurse**, or drink milk from its mother. Calves often nurse underwater.

FAST FACT

Hippos can sleep underwater. They bob to the surface to take breaths without waking up!

A calf can spend up to 16 hours a day in the water. They even sleep in it!

KEEPING COOL

Hippos live in Africa. Calves spend their days near their mother in **shallow** water. Rivers and lakes keep them cool in the African heat.

FAST FACT

Newborn calves can only hold their breath underwater for less than a minute. Adults can hold their breath for up to five minutes!

A cow and calf walk across shallow water in Africa.

LEAVING THE WATER

When the calf is strong enough, it can leave the water. It usually leaves after the sun goes down. The cow and calf head to land to **graze**.

FAST FACT

Calves cannot sleep without their mothers!

A cow and her calf walk along pathways to graze.

HUNGRY HIPPOS

Calves will eat grasses and plants. If they find fruit, they will eat that, too. Sometimes they must travel a long distance to find food.

FAST FACT

The calf uses its lips for pulling out the grass and its back teeth for chewing.

A hippo can eat about 80 pounds (36 kilograms) of grass! That sounds like a lot, but it's not much for such a huge animal.

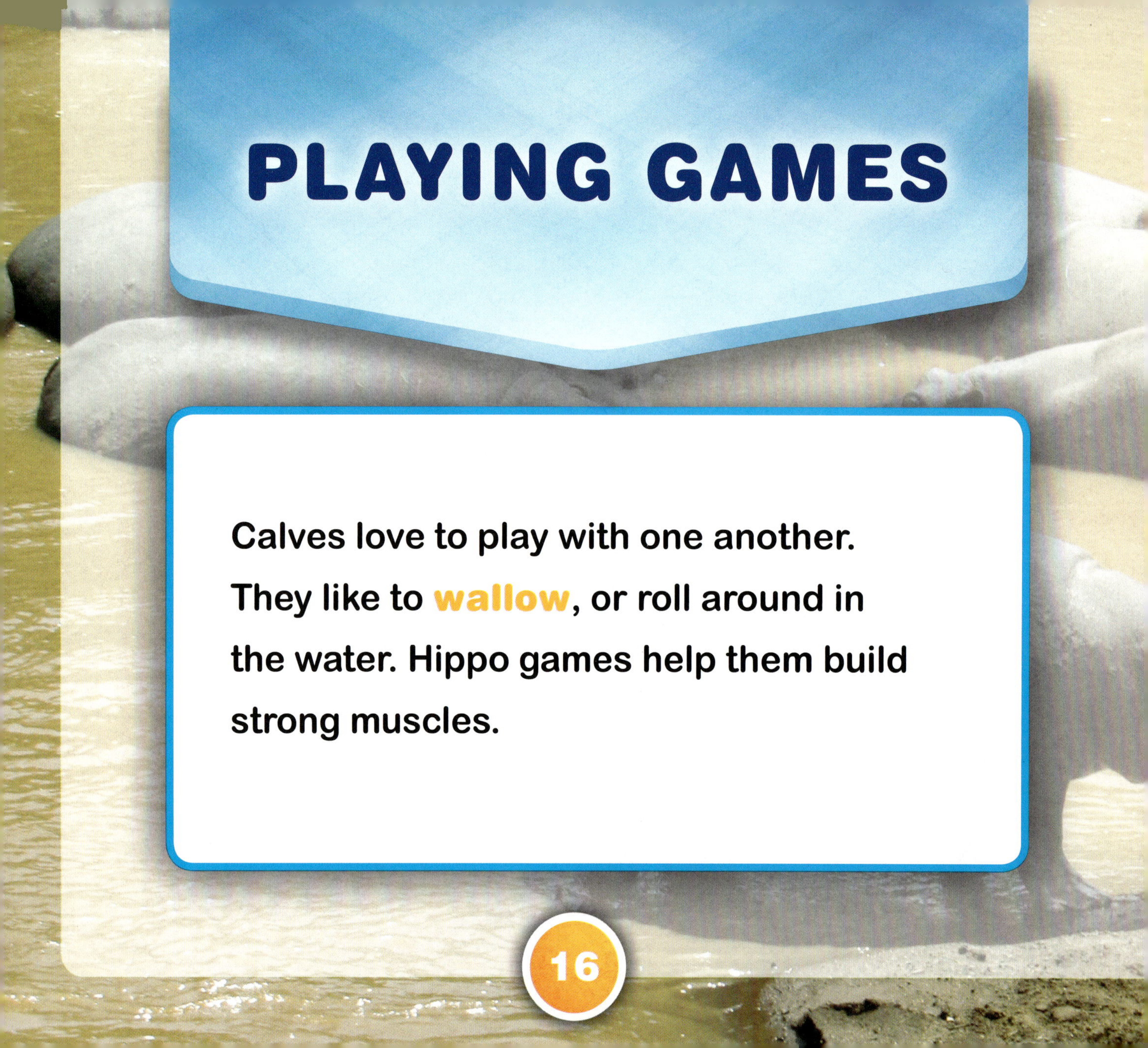

PLAYING GAMES

Calves love to play with one another. They like to **wallow**, or roll around in the water. Hippo games help them build strong muscles.

FAST FACT

Calves will grow to be one of the largest land animals on Earth.

Calves play-fight in the water. This is practice for when they become adults and have to fight for real.

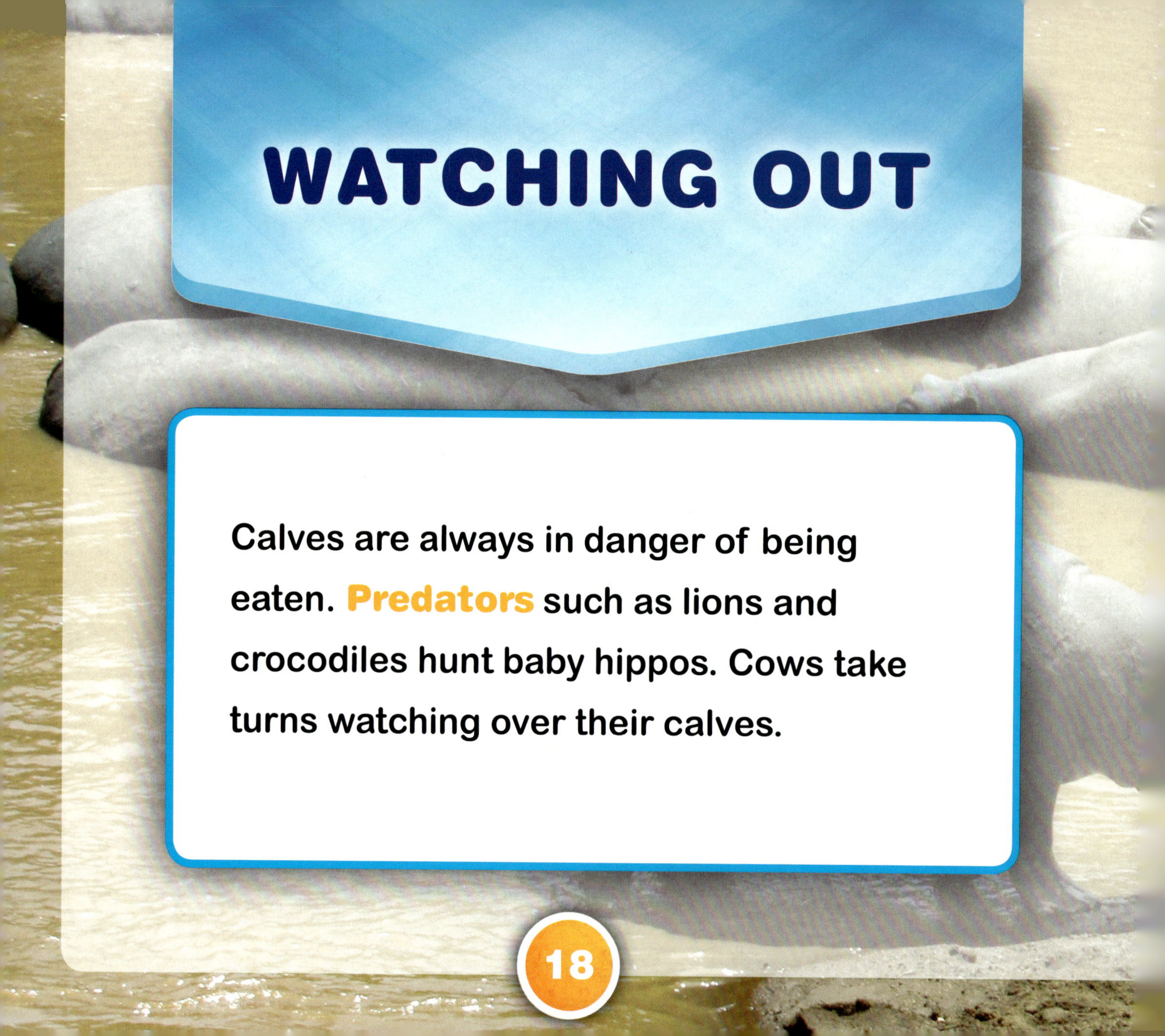

WATCHING OUT

Calves are always in danger of being eaten. **Predators** such as lions and crocodiles hunt baby hippos. Cows take turns watching over their calves.

A cow opens her mouth wide to scare off any animal that may want to hurt her calf.

FAST FACT

Calves can sometimes be hurt when caught in the middle of fighting hippos.

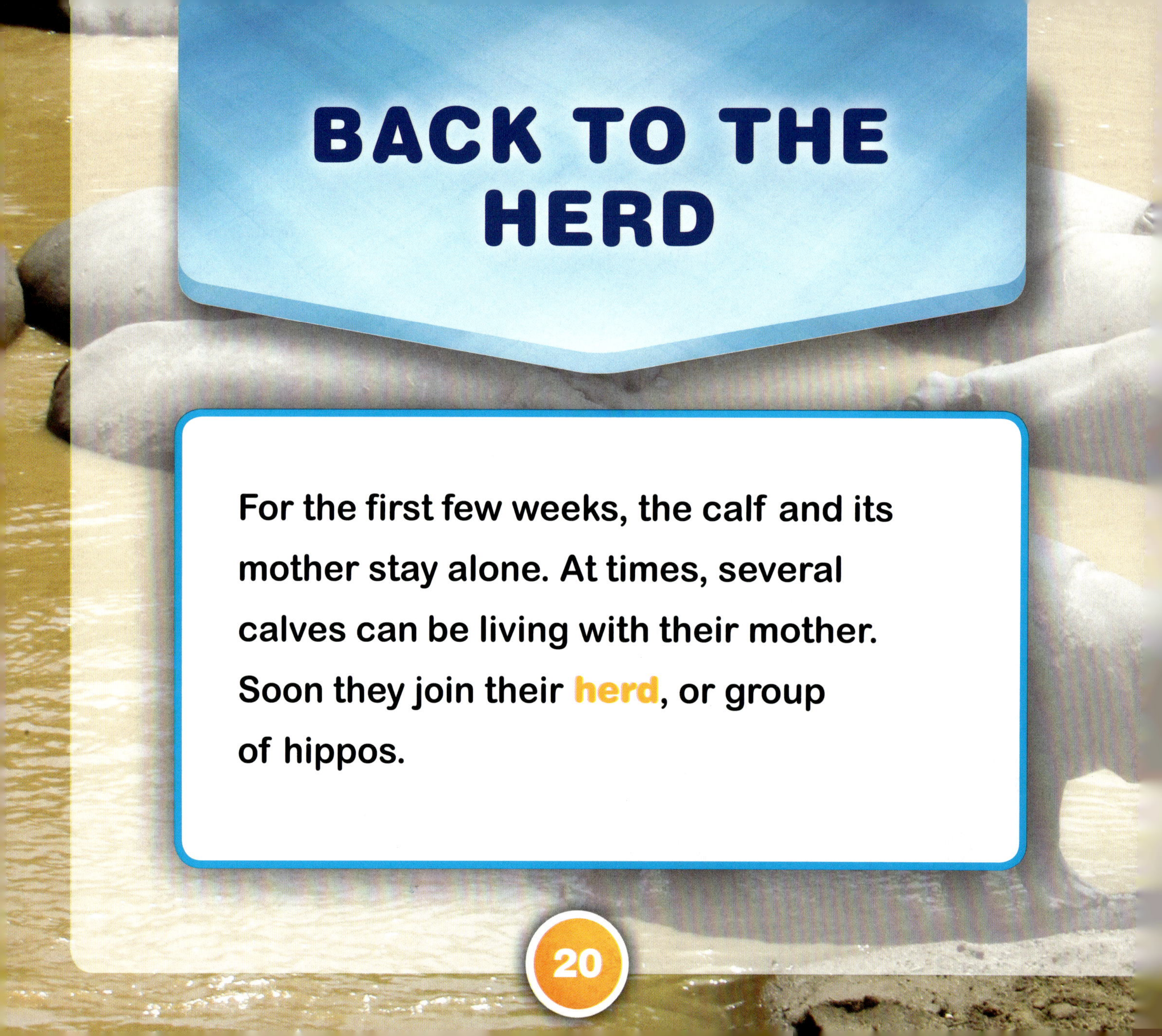

BACK TO THE HERD

For the first few weeks, the calf and its mother stay alone. At times, several calves can be living with their mother. Soon they join their **herd**, or group of hippos.

FAST FACT

Hippos can talk to each other underwater.

Being part of a herd helps keep the calves safe from predators.

LEAVING MOTHER

Some calves will leave their mother at one year old. Others will stay with her for as long as four years. Females can have their own babies at five or six years old. Males can **breed** at seven or eight years old.

For the next few years, a cow will teach her calf how to survive in the wild.

FAST FACT

Hippos may live as long as 30 years in nature.

LEARN MORE

Books

Klukow, Mary Ellen. *Hippos*. Mankato, MN: Amicus Ink, 2019.

Maynard, Thane. *Saving Fiona: The Story of the World's Most Famous Baby Hippo*. Boston, MA: Houghton, Mifflin, Harcourt, 2018.

Owings, Lisa. *Meet a Baby Hippo*. Minneapolis, MN: Learner Publishing Group, 2015.

Websites

National Geographic Kids: Hippopotamus
kids.nationalgeographic.com/animals/hippopotamus/
Find out how a hippo can breathe, see, and even hear while it's body is underwater!

San Diego Zoo Kids: Hippopotamus
animals.sandiegozoo.org/animals/hippo
Learn more about one of the largest animals on Earth.

INDEX

Published in 2020 by Enslow Publishing, LLC
101 W. 23rd Street, Suite 240, New York, NY 10011

Library of Congress Cataloging-in-Publication Data

Names: Bozzo, Linda, author.
Title: How hippos grow up / Linda Bozzo.
Description: New York : Enslow Publishing, 2020. | Series: Animals growing up | Includes bibliographical references and index. | Audience: K to Grade 3.
Identifiers: LCCN 2019004358| ISBN 9781978512351 (library bound) | ISBN 9781978512337 (paperback) | ISBN 9781978512344 (6 pack)
Subjects: LCSH: Hippopotamidae—Development—Juvenile literature. | Hippopotamidae—Infancy—Juvenile literature.
Classification: LCC QL737.U57 B69 2020 | DDC 599.63/5—dc23
LC record available at https://lccn.loc.gov/2019004358

Printed in the United States of America

To Our Readers: We have done our best to make sure all website addresses in this book were active and appropriate when we went to press. However, the author and the publisher have no control over and assume no liability for the material available on those websites or on any websites they may link to. Any comments or suggestions can be sent by email to customerservice@enslow.com.

Photos Credits: Cover, p. 1 Netta Arobas/Shutterstock.com; interior pages 4-23 (background), p. 21 Geoffrey Kuchera/Shutterstock.com; p. 5 lumendigital/ Shutterstock.com; p. 7 Little Things Abroad/Shutterstock.com; p. 9 topimages/ Shutterstock.com; p. 11 Vicki Jauron, Babylon and Beyond Photography/Moment/ Getty Images; p. 13 Stephan Raats/Shutterstock.com; p. 15 Lindsey Stevens/ Shutterstock.com; p. 17 Enn Li Photography/Moment/Getty Images; p. 19 SJ Watt/Shutterstock.com; p. 23 Henk Bogaard/Shutterstock.com; back cover and additional interior pages background graphic 13Imagery/Shutterstock.com.